W9-CEV-577

POEMS

1938 - 1945

POEMS

1938-1945

By

Robert Graves, *1895-*

FARRAR, STRAUS & GIROUX
NEW YORK

BRIAR CLIFF COLLEGE
LIBRARY
SIOUX CITY, IOWA

Copyright 1946 by Robert Graves
All rights reserved
Library of Congress catalog card number: 46-5047

First Creative Age Press edition, 1946
First Farrar, Straus and Giroux edition, 1967
Printed in the United States of America

PR
6013
. R35
P6
1946a

FOREWORD

———

Since poems should be self-explanatory I refrain from more foreword than this: that I write poems for poets, and satires or grotesques for wits. For people in general I write prose, and am content that they should be unaware that I do anything else. To write poems for other than poets is wasteful. The moral of the Scilly Islanders who earned a precarious livelihood by taking in one another's washing is that they never upset their carefully balanced island economy by trying to horn into the laundry trade of the mainland; and that nowhere in the Western Hemisphere was washing so well done.

Galmpton- Brixham,   R. G.
S. Devon.

1945.

50721

CONTENTS

Poems

Satires and Grotesques

POEMS

A LOVE STORY

———

The full moon easterly rising, furious,
Against a winter sky ragged with red;
The hedges high in snow, and owls raving—
Solemnities not easy to withstand:
A shiver wakes the spine.

In boyhood, having encountered the scene,
I suffered horror: I fetched the moon home,
With owls and snow, to nurse in my head
Throughout the trials of a new spring,
Famine unassuaged.

But fell in love, and made a lodgement
Of love on those frozen ramparts.
Her image was my ensign: snows melted,
Hedges sprouted, the moon tenderly shone,
The owls trilled with tongues of nightingale.

These were all lies, though they matched the time,
And brought me less than luck: her image
Warped in the weather, turned beldamish.
Then back came winter on me at a bound,
The pallid sky heaved with a moon-quake.

3

Dangerous it had been with love-notes
To serenade Queen Famine.
In tears I recomposed the former scene,
Let the snow lie, watched the moon rise, suffered the
owls,
Paid homage to them of unevent.

DAWN BOMBARDMENT

———

Guns from the sea open against us:
The smoke rocks bodily in the casemate
And a yell of doom goes up.
We count and bless each new, heavy concussion—
Captives awaiting rescue.

Visiting angel of the wild-fire hair
Who in dream reassured us nightly
Where we lay fettered,
Laugh at us, as we wake—our faces
So tense with hope the tears run down.

THE WORMS OF HISTORY

On the eighth day God died: his bearded mouth
That had been shut so long flew open.
So Adam's too in a dismay like death—
But the world still rolled on around him,
Instinct with all those lesser powers of life
That God had groaned against but not annulled.

"All-excellent," Adam had titled God,
And in his mourning now demeaned himself
As if all excellence, not God, had died;
Chose to be governed by those lesser powers,
More than inferior to excellence—
The worms astir in God's corrupt flesh.

God died, not excellence his name:
Excellence lived but only was not God.
It was those lesser powers who played at God,
Bloated with Adam's deferential sighs
Which were his mourning for divinity:
They reigned as royal monsters upon earth.

Adam grew lean, and wore perpetual black;
He made no reaching after excellence.
Eve gave him sorry comfort for his grief
With birth of sons, and mourning still he died.
Adam was buried in one grave with God
And the worms ranged and ravaged in between.

Into their white maws fell abundance
Of all things rotten. They were greedy-nosed
To smell the taint out and go scavenging,
Yet over excellence held no domain.
Excellence lives; they are already dead—
The ages of a putrefying corpse.

THE BEAST

———

Beyond the Atlas roams a love-beast;
The aborigines harry it with darts;
Its flesh is esteemed, though of a fishy tang
Tainting the eater's mouth and lips.
Ourselves once, wandering in mid-wilderness
And by despair drawn to this diet,
Before the meal was over sat apart
Loathing each other's carrion company.

A WITHERING HERB

——

Ambition in the herb denied his root.
In dreams of the dark he whispered:
"O to be all flower, and to star the sky—
True brother to the moon, that stalkless flower
Who long has cherished me!"

Disdained the happy sun of morning,
Held it gross rival to the sovereign moon—
Thus for ambition cast his cloak of leaves
Yet could not snap the stalk, to float upward
And from his roots be free:
So withered staunchly.

THE SHOT

———

The curious heart plays with its fears:
To hurl a shot through the ship's planks,
Being assured that the green angry flood
Is charmed, it dares not dance into the hold—
Nor first to sweep a lingering glance around
For land or shoal or cask adrift.
"So miracles are done; but madmen drown."

O weary luxury of hypothesis—
For human nature, honest human nature
(Which the fear-pampered heart denies)
Knows its own miracle: not to go mad.
Will pitch the shot in fancy, hint the fact,
Will bore perhaps a meagre auger hole
But stanch the spurting with a tarred rag,
And will not drown, nor even ride the cask.

THE THIEVES

————

Lovers in the act dispense
With such meum-teum sense
As might warningly reveal
What they must not pick or steal,
And their nostrum is to say:
I and you are both away.

After, when they disentwine
You from me and yours from mine,
Neither can be certain who
Was that I whose mine was you.
To the act again they go
More completely not to know.

Theft is theft and raid is raid
Though reciprocally made.
Lovers, the conclusion is
Doubled sighs and jealousies
In a single heart that grieves
For lost honour among thieves.

LOLLOCKS

———

By sloth on sorrow fathered
These dusty-featured Lollocks
Have their nativity in all disordered
Backs of cupboard drawers.

They play hide and seek
Among collars and novels
And empty medicine bottles,
And letters from abroad
That never will be answered.

Every sultry night
They plague little children,
Gurgling from the cistern,
Humming from the air,
Skewing up the bed-clothes,
Twitching the blind.

When the imbecile agèd
Are over-long in dying
And the nurse drowses,

Lollocks come skipping
Up the tattered stairs
And are nasty together
In the bed's shadow.

The signs of their presence
Are boils on the neck,
Dreams of vexation suddenly recalled
In the middle of the morning,
Languor after food.

Men cannot see them,
Men cannot hear them,
Do not believe in them—
But suffer the more,
Both in neck and belly.

Women can see them—
O those naughty wives
Who sit by the fireside
Munching bread and honey,
Watching them in mischief
From corners of their eyes,
Slily allowing them to lick
Honey-sticky fingers.

Sovereign against Lollocks
Are hard broom and soft broom,

To well comb the hair,
To well brush the shoe,
And to pay every debt
So soon as it's due.

TO SLEEP

The mind's eye sees as the heart mirrors:
Loving in part, I did not see you whole,
Grew flesh-enraged that I could not conjure
A whole you to attend my fever-fit
In the doubtful hour between a night and day
And be Sleep that had been so long away.

Of you sometimes a hand, a brooch, a shoe
Wavered beside me, unarticulated—
As the vexed insomniac dream-forges;
And the words I chose for your voice to speak
Echoed my own voice with its dry creak.

Now that I love you, now that I recall
All scattered elements of will that swooped
By night as jealous dreams through windows
To circle above the beds like bats,
Or as dawn birds flew blindly at the panes
In curiosity rattling out their brains—

Now that I love you, as not before,
Now you can be and say, as not before:
The mind clears and the heart true-mirrors you
Where at my side an early watch you keep
And all self-bruising heads loll into sleep.

DESPITE AND STILL

Have you not read
The words in my head,
And I made part
Of your own heart?
We have been such as draw
The losing straw—
You of your gentleness,
I of my rashness,
Both of despair—
Yet still might share
This happy will:
To love despite and still.
Never let us deny
The thing's necessity,
But, O, refuse
To choose
Where chance may seem to give
Loves in alternative.

THE SUICIDE IN THE COPSE

The suicide, far from content,
Stared down at his own shattered skull:
Was this what he meant?

Had not his purpose been
To liberate himself from duns and dolts
By a change of scene?

From somewhere came a roll of laughter:
He had looked so on his wedding-day,
And the day after.

There was nowhere at all to go,
And no diversion now but to peruse
What literature the winds might blow

Into the copse where his body lay—
A year-old sheet of sporting news,
A crumpled schoolboy essay.

FRIGHTENED MEN

———

We are not of their kind, nor ever were,
Never having had such claws to our paws
In any hypothetic incarnation;
Have only the least knowledge of their minds
Through a grace on their part in thinking aloud;
And we remain mouse-quiet when they begin
Suddenly in their unpredictable way
To weave an allegory of their lives,
Making each point by walking round it—
Then off again, as interest is warmed.
What have they said? Or unsaid? What?
We understood the general drift only.

They are punctilious as implacable,
Most amiable with those who hate them most.
A shout will scare them. When they spring, they
  seize.
The worst is when they hide from us and change
To something altogether other:
We meet them at the door, as who returns
After a one-hour-seeming century
To a house not his own.

19

A STRANGER AT THE PARTY

For annoyance, not shame,
   Under their covert stares
She would not give her name
   Nor demand theirs.

Soon everyone at the party,
   Who knew everyone,
Eyed her with plain envy
   For knowing none—

Such neighbourly mistrust
   Breathed across the floor,
Such familiar disgust
   With what they were and wore—

Until, as she was leaving,
   Her time out-stayed,
They tried to say they loved her;
   But pride forbade.

THE OATH

———

The doubt and the passion
Falling away from them,
   In that instant both
Take timely courage
From the sky's clearness
   To confirm an oath.

Her loves are his loves,
His trust is her trust;
   Else all were grief
And they, lost travellers
On a yellowing page,
   Death overleaf.

Rumour of old battle
Growls across the air;
   Then let it growl
With no more terror
Than the creaking stair
   Or the calling owl.

She knows, as he knows,
Of a faithful-always

And an always-dear
By early emblems
Prognosticated,
    Fulfilled here.

LANGUAGE OF THE SEASONS

Living among orchards, we are ruled
By the four seasons necessarily:
This from unseasonable frosts we learn
Or from usurping suns and haggard flowers—
Legitimist our disapproval.

Weather we knew, not seasons, in the city
While, seasonless, orange and orchid shone,
Knew it by heavy overcoat or light,
Framed love in later terminologies
Than here, where we report how weight of snow,
Or weight of fruit, tears branches from the tree.

MID-WINTER WAKING

———

Stirring suddenly from long hibernation
I knew myself once more a poet
Guarded by timeless principalities
Against the worm of death, this hillside haunting;
And presently dared open both my eyes.

O gracious, lofty, shone against from under,
Back-of-the-mind-far clouds like towers;
And you, sudden warm airs that blow
Before the expected season of new blossom,
While sheep still gnaw at roots and lambless go—

Be witness that on waking, this mid-winter,
I found her hand in mine laid closely
Who shall watch out the Spring with me.
We stared in silence all around us
But found no winter anywhere to see.

THE ROCK AT THE CORNER

———

The quarrymen left ragged
A rock at the corner;
But over it move now
The comforting fingers
Of ivy and briar.

Nor will it need assurance
Of nature's compassion
When presently it weathers
To a noble landmark
Of such countenance

That travellers in winter
Will know it for a creature
On guard at the corner
Where deep snows ingratiate
The comforts of death.

THE BEACH

———

Louder than gulls the little children scream
Whom fathers haul into the jovial foam,
But others fearlessly rush in, breast high,
Laughing the salty water from their mouths—
Heroes of the nursery.

The horny boatman, who has seen whales
And flying fishes, who has sailed as far
As Demerara and the Ivory Coast,
Will warn them, when they crowd to hear his tales,
That every ocean smells alike of tar.

THE VILLAGERS AND DEATH

———

The Rector's pallid neighbour at The Firs,
Death, did not flurry the parishioners.
Yet from a weight of superstitious fears
Each tried to lengthen his own term of years.
He was congratulated who combined
Toughness of flesh and weakness of the mind
In consequential rosiness of face.
This dull, and not ill-mannered, populace
Pulled off their caps to Death, as they slouched by,
But rumoured him both atheist and spy.
All vowed to outlast him (though none ever did)
And hear the earth drum on his coffin-lid.
Their groans and whispers down the village street
Soon soured his nature, which was never sweet.

THE DOOR

———

When she came suddenly in
It seemed the door could never close again,
Nor even did she close it—she, she—
The room lay open to a visiting sea
That no door could restrain.

Yet when at last she smiled, tilting her head
To take her leave of me,
Where she had smiled, instead
There was a dark door closing endlessly,
The waves receded.

UNDER THE POT

———

Sulkily the sticks burn, and though they crackle
   With scorn under the bubbling pot, or spout
Magnanimous jets of flame against the smoke,
   At each heel end a dirty sap runs out.

Confess, creatures, how sulkily ourselves
   We hiss with doom, fuel of a sodden age—
Not rapt up roaring to the chimney stack
   On incandescent clouds of spirit or rage.

THROUGH NIGHTMARE

———

Never be disenchanted of
That place you sometimes dream yourself into,
Lying at large remove beyond all dream,
Or those you find there, though but seldom
In their company seated—

The untameable, the live, the gentle.
Have you not known them? Whom? They carry
Time looped so river-wise about their house,
There's no way in by history's road
To name or number them.

In your sleepy eyes I read the journey
Of which disjointedly you tell; which stirs
My loving admiration, that you should travel
Through nightmare to a lost and moated land,
Who are timorous by nature.

TO LUCIA AT BIRTH

———

Though the moon beaming matronly and bland
   Greets you, among the crowd of the new-born,
With "welcome to the world," yet understand
   That still her pale, lascivious unicorn
And bloody lion are loose on either hand:
   With din of bones and tantarará of horn
Their fanciful cortege parades the land—
   Pest on the high road, wild-fire in the corn.

Outrageous company to be born into,
   Lunatics of a shining age long dead.
Then reckon time by what you are or do,
   Not by the epochs of the war they spread.
   Hark how they roar; but never turn your head.
Nothing will change them, let them not change you.

DEATH BY DRUMS

———

Did I cry out in anger against music,
    It was not that I cried
Against the pure and wholesome arsenic
    Necessary for suicide—
For suicide in the drums' racking riot
    Where horned moriscoes wailing to their bride
Scare every Lydian songster from the spot.

SHE TELLS HER LOVE WHILE HALF-ASLEEP

———

She tells her love while half-asleep,
In the dark hours,
With half-words whispered low:
As Earth stirs in her winter sleep
And puts out grass and flowers
Despite the snow,
Despite the falling snow.

INSTRUCTIONS TO THE ORPHIC ADEPT

———

So soon as ever your mazed spirit descends
From daylight into darkness, Man, remember
What you have suffered here in Samothrace,
What you have suffered.

After your passage through Hell's seven floods,
Whose fumes of sulphur will have parched your
    throat,
The Halls of Judgement shall loom up before you,
A miracle of jasper and of onyx.
To the left hand there bubbles a black spring
Overshadowed with a great white cypress.
Avoid this spring, which is Forgetfulness;
Though all the common rout rush down to drink,
Avoid this spring.

To the right hand there lies a secret pool
Alive with speckled trout and fish of gold;
A hazel overshadows it; Ophion,
Primaeval serpent straggling in the branches,
Darts out his tongue. This holy pool is fed
By dripping water; guardians stand before it.

34

Run to this pool, the pool of Memory,
Run to this pool.

Then will the guardians scrutinize you, saying:
"Who are you, who? What have you to remember?
Do you not fear Ophion's flickering tongue?
Go rather to the spring beneath the cypress,
Flee from this pool."

Then you shall answer: "I am parched with thirst.
Give me to drink. I am a child of Earth,
But of Sky also, come from Samothrace.
Witness the glint of amber on my brow.
Out of the Pure I come, as you may see.
I also am of your thrice-blessèd kin,
Child of the three-fold Queen of Samothrace;
Have made full quittance for my deeds of blood,
Have been by her invested in sea-purple,
And like a kid have fallen into milk.
Give me to drink, now I am parched with thirst,
Give me to drink!"

But they will ask you yet: "What of your feet?"
You shall reply: "My feet have borne me here
Out of the weary wheel, the circling years,
To that still, spokeless wheel:—Persephone.
Give me to drink!"

Then they will welcome you with fruit and flowers,
And lead you toward the ancient dripping hazel,
Crying: "Brother of our immortal blood,
Drink and remember glorious Samothrace!"
Then you shall drink.

You shall drink deep of that refreshing draught,
To become lords of the uninitiated
Twittering ghosts, Hell's countless populace—
To become heroes, knights upon swift horses,
Pronouncing oracles from tall white tombs,
By the nymphs tended. They with honey water
Shall pour libations to your serpent shapes,
That you may drink.

THESEUS AND ARIADNE

———

High on his figured couch beyond the waves
He dreams, in dream recalling her set walk
Down paths of oyster-shell bordered with flowers
And down the shadowy turf beneath the vine.
He sighs: "Deep sunk in my erroneous past
She haunts the ruins and the ravaged lawns."

Yet still unharmed it stands, the regal house
Crooked with age and overtopped by pines
Where first he wearied of her constancy.
And with a surer foot she goes than when
Dread of his hate was thunder in the air,
When the pines agonized with flaws of wind
And flowers glared up at her with frantic eyes.
Of him, now all is done, she never dreams
But calls a living blessing down upon
What he would have mere rubble and rank grass;
Playing the queen to nobler company.

LAMENT FOR PASIPHAË

———

Dying sun, shine warm a little longer!
My eye, dazzled with tears, shall dazzle yours,
Conjuring you to shine and not to move.
You, sun, and I all afternoon have laboured
Beneath a dewless and oppressive cloud—
A fleece now gilded with our common grief
That this must be a night without a moon.
Dying sun, shine warm a little longer!

Faithless she was not: she was very woman,
Smiling with dire impartiality,
Sovereign, with heart unmatched, adored of men,
Until Spring's cuckoo with bedraggled plumes
Tempted her pity and her truth betrayed.
Then she who shone for all resigned her being,
And this must be a night without a moon.
Dying sun, shine warm a little longer!

THE TWELVE DAYS OF CHRISTMAS

———

The outrageous child who stole the axe of power,
Debauched his virgin mother
And fiercely vowed he would be God the Father—

Senile and fat the way of all flesh goes:
Into the kitchen where roast goose,
Plum-pudding and mince-pies his red robes grease.

She from the tree-top, true to her deserts,
With wand and silver skirts
Presides unravished over all pure hearts.

COLD WEATHER PROVERB

———

Fearless approach and puffed feather
In birds, famine bespeak;
In man, belly filled full.

TO JUAN AT THE WINTER SOLSTICE

There is one story and one story only
That will prove worth your telling,
Whether as learned bard or gifted child;
To it all lines or lesser gauds belong
That startle with their shining
Such common stories as they stray into.

Is it of trees you tell, their months and virtues,
Of strange beasts that beset you,
Of birds that croak at you the Triple will?
Or of the Zodiac and how slow it turns
Below the Boreal Crown,
Prison of all true kings that ever reigned?

Water to water, ark again to ark,
From woman back to woman:
So each new victim treads unfalteringly
The never altered circuit of his fate,
Bringing twelve peers as witness
Both to his starry rise and starry fall.

Or is it of the Virgin's silver beauty,
All fish below the thighs?
She in her left hand bears a leafy quince;
When with her right she crooks a finger, smiling,
How may the King hold back?
Royally then he barters life for love.

Or of the undying snake from chaos hatched,
Whose coils contain the ocean,
Into whose chops with naked sword he springs,
Then in black water, tangled by the reeds,
Battles three days and nights,
To be spewed up beside her scalloped shore?

Much snow is falling, winds roar hollowly,
The owl hoots from the elder,
Fear in your heart cries to the loving-cup:
Sorrow to sorrow as the sparks fly upward.
The log groans and confesses
There is one story and one story only.

Dwell on her graciousness, dwell on her smiling,
Do not forget what flowers
The great boar trampled down in ivy time.
Her brow was creamy as the long ninth wave,
Her sea-blue eyes were wild
But nothing promised that is not performed.

SATIRES AND GROTESQUES

DREAM OF A CLIMBER

———

Watch how this climber raises his own ladder
From earth to heaven, and not in a night
Nor from the secret, stony pillow.
(World patents pending; tested in the shops.)

Here's quality timber, nosings of pure brass,
The perfect phallo-spiritual tilt,
A fuzzy puff of cloud on top—
Excellent lure for angels and archangels!

Come, climber, with your scientific hat
And beady gambler's eye, ascend!
He pauses, poses for his camera-man:
"Well-known Climber About to Ascend."

But in the published print, we may be sure,
He will appear, not on the lowest rung
But nearly out of view, almost in the cloud,
Leaning aside for an angel to pass,
His muscular broad hands a-glint in the sun,
And crampons on his feet.

THE PERSIAN VERSION

———

Truth-loving Persians do not dwell upon
The trivial skirmish fought near Marathon.
As for the Greek theatrical tradition
Which represents that summer's expedition
Not as a mere reconnaissance in force
By three brigades of foot and one of horse
(Their left flank covered by some obsolete
Light craft detached from the main Persian fleet)
But as a grandiose, ill-starred attempt
To conquer Greece—they treat it with contempt;
And only incidentally refute
Major Greek claims, by stressing what repute
The Persian monarch and the Persian nation
Won by this salutary demonstration:
Despite a strong defence and adverse weather
All arms combined magnificently together.

THE WEATHER OF OLYMPUS

———

Zeus was once overheard to shout at Hera:
    "You hate it, do you? Well, I hate it worse—
Boreas all May, Sirocco all the Summer.
    Hell take this whole impossible Universe!"

A scholiast explains this warm rejoinder
    Which seems too manlike for Olympic use,
By noting that the snake-tailed Chthonian winds
    Were answerable to Fate alone, not Zeus.

APOLLO OF THE PHYSIOLOGISTS

———

Despite this learned cult's official
And seemingly sincere denial
That they either reject or postulate
God, or God's scientific surrogate,
Prints of a deity occur *passim*
Throughout their extant literature: they make him
A dumb, dead-pan Apollo with a profile
Drawn in Victorian-Hellenistic style—
The pallid, bald, partitioned head suggesting
Wholly abstract cerebral functioning,
Or nude and at full length, this deity
Displays digestive, venous, respiratory
And nervous systems painted in bold colour
On his immaculate exterior.
Sometimes, *in verso,* a bald, naked Muse,
His consort, flaunts her arteries and sinews,
While, upside-down, crouched on her chaste abdo-
    men,
Adored by men and wondered at by women,
Hangs a Victorian-Hellenistic foetus—
Fruit of her academic god's afflatus.

THE OLDEST SOLDIER

The sun shines warm on seven old soldiers
    Paraded in a row,
Perched like starlings on the railings—
    Give them plug-tobacco!

They'll croon you the Oldest-Soldier Song,
    Of Harry who took a holiday
From the sweat of ever thinking for himself
    Or going his own bloody way.

It was arms-drill, guard and kit-inspection,
    Like dreams of a long train-journey,
And the barrack-bed that Harry dossed on
    Went rockabye, rockabye, rockabye.

Harry kept his rifle and brasses clean,
    But Jesus Christ, what a liar!
He won the Military Medal
    For his coolness under fire.

49

He was never the last on parade
　　Nor the first to volunteer,
And when Harry rose to be storeman
　　He seldom had to pay for his beer.

Twenty-one years, and out Harry came
　　To be odd-job man, or janitor,
Or commissionaire at a picture-house,
　　Or, some say, bully to a whore.

But his King and Country calling Harry,
　　He reported again at the Depôt,
To perch on this railing like a starling,
　　The oldest soldier in the row.

GROTESQUES

———

I

My Chinese uncle, gouty, deaf, half-blinded,
And more than a trifle absent-minded,
Astonished all St. James's Square one day
By giving long and unexceptionably exact directions
To a little coolie girl, who'd lost her way.

II

The Lion-faced Boy at the Fair
And the Heir Apparent
Were equally slow at remembering people's faces.
But whenever they met, incognito, in the Brazilian
Pavilion, the Row and such-like places,
They exchanged, it is said, their sternest nods
Like gods of dissimilar races.

III

Dr. Newman with the crooked pince-nez
Had studied in Vienna and Chicago.
Chess was his only relaxation.

And Dr. Newman remained unperturbed
By every nastier manifestation
Of plutodemocratic civilization:
All that was cranky, corny, ill-behaved,
Unnecessary, askew or orgiastic
Would creep unbidden to his side-door (hidden
Behind a poster in the Tube Station
Nearly half-way up the moving-stairs)
Push its way in, to squat there undisturbed
Among box files and tubular steel chairs.

He was once seen at the Philharmonic Hall
Noting the reactions of two patients,
With pronounced paranoiac tendencies,
To old Dutch music. He appeared to recall
A tin of lozenges in his breast-pocket,
Put his hand confidently in—
And drew out a black imp, or sooterkin,
Six inches long, with one ear upside-down,
Licking at a vanilla ice-cream cornet—
Then put it back again with a slight frown.

IV

A Royal Duke, with no campaigning medals
To dignify his Orders, he would speak
Nostalgically at times of Mozambique
Where once the ship he cruised in ran aground:

How he drank cocoa, from a sailor's mug,
Poured from the common jug,
While loyal toasts went round.

V

Sir John addressed the Snake God in his temple,
Which was full of bats, not as a votary
But with the somewhat cynical courtesy,
Just short of condescension,
He might have paid the Governor-General
Of a small, hot, backward colony.
He was well versed in primitive religion,
But found this an embarrassing occasion:
The God was immense, noisy and affable,
Began to tickle him with a nervous chuckle,
Unfobbed a great gold clock for him to listen,
Hissed like a snake, and swallowed him at one
    mouthful.

THE EUGENIST

———

Come, human dogs, interfertilitate—
    Blackfellow and white lord, brown, yellow and
      red!
Accept the challenge of the lately bred
    Newfoundland terrier with the dachshund gait.*

Breed me gigantic pygmies, meek-eyed Scots,
    Phlegmatic Irish, perfume-hating Poles,
Poker-faced, toothy, pigtailed Hottentots,
    And Germans with no envy in their souls.

* See: Charles R. Stockard and collaborators: *The genetic and endocrinic basis for differences in form and behavior, as elucidated by studies of contrasted pure-line dogbreeds and their hybrids.* (Philadelphia, 1941.)

1805

———

At Viscount Nelson's lavish funeral,
    While the mob milled and yelled about the Abbey,
A General chatted with an Admiral:

"One of your Colleagues, Sir, remarked today
    That Nelson's *exit*, though to be lamented,
Falls not inopportunely, in its way."

"He was a thorn in our flesh," came the reply—
    "The most bird-witted, unaccountable,
Odd little runt that ever I did spy.

"One arm, one peeper, vain as Pretty Poll,
    A meddler, too, in foreign politics
And gave his heart in pawn to a plain moll.

"He would dare lecture us Sea Lords, and then
    Would treat his ratings as though men of honour
And play at leap-frog with his midshipmen!

"We tried to box him down, but up he popped,
    And when he'd banged Napoleon at the Nile
Became too much the hero to be dropped.

"You've heard that Copenhagen 'blind eye' story?
    We'd tied him to Nurse Parker's apron-strings
By G——d, he snipped them through and snatched
    the glory!"

"Yet," cried the General, "six-and-twenty sail
    Captured or sunk by him off Tráfalgar—
That writes a handsome *finis* to the tale."

"Handsome enough. The seas are England's now.
    That fellow's foibles need no longer plague us.
He died most creditably, I'll allow."

"And, Sir, the secret of his victories?"
    "By his unServicelike, familiar ways, Sir,
He made the whole Fleet love him, damn his eyes!"

AT THE SAVOY CHAPEL

(From *World's Press News,* February 22, 1945: "Alexander
Clifford, the war correspondent, is today marrying Flight Officer
Jenny Nicholson, daughter of Robert Graves. They met in the
front line.")

———

Up to the wedding, formal with heir-loom lace,
Press-cameras, carnations out of season,
Well-mellowed priest and well-trained choristers,

The relatives come marching, such as meet
Only at weddings and at funerals,
The elder generation with the eldest.

Family features for years undecided
What look to wear against a loveless world
Fix, as the wind veers, in the same grimace.

Each eyes the others with a furtive pity:
"Heavens, how she has aged—and he,
Grey hair and sunken cheeks, what a changed man!"

They stare wistfully at the bride (released
From brass buttons and the absurd salute)
In long white gown, bouquet and woman's pride.

"How suitable!" they whisper, and the whisper
"How suitable!" rustles from pew to pew;
To which I nod suitable grave assent.

Now for you, loving ones, who kneel at the altar
And preside afterwards at table—
The trophy sword that shears the cake recalling

What god you entertained last year together,
His bull neck looped with guts,
Trampling corpse-carpet through the villages—

Here is my private blessing: so to remain
As today you are, with features
Resolute and unchangeably your own.